This book belongs to:

____

Made in the USA
Coppell, TX
02 December 2022

87642169R00063